Snacks for Healthy Teeth

by Mari Schuh

Consulting Editor:
Gail Saunders-Smith, PhD

Consultant:
Lori Gagliardi CDA, RDA, RDH, EdD

Capstone press®

Mankato, Minnesota

Pebble Plus is published by Capstone Press,
151 Good Counsel Drive, P.O. Box 669, Mankato, Minnesota 56002.
www.capstonepress.com

1 2 3 4 5 6 13 12 11 10 09 08

Library of Congress Cataloging-in-Publication Data
Schuh, Mari C., 1975–
    Snacks for healthy teeth/by Mari Schuh.
    p. cm. — (Pebble plus. Healthy teeth)
    Summary: "Simple text, photographs, and diagrams present information about healthy snacks for teeth
and includes how to take care of teeth properly" — Provided by publisher.
    Includes bibliographical references and index.
    ISBN-13: 978-1-4296-1239-5 (hardcover)
    ISBN-10: 1-4296-1239-8 (hardcover)
    ISBN-13: 978-1-4296-1785-7 (softcover)
    ISBN-10: 1-4296-1785-3 (softcover)
    1. Nutrition and dental health — Juvenile literature. I. Title. II. Series.
RK281.S29 2008
617.6'01 — dc22
                                                        2007027116

Editorial Credits
Sarah L. Schuette, editor; Veronica Bianchini, designer and illustrator

Photo Credits
Capstone Press/Karon Dubke, all

The author dedicates this book to her husband, Joseph Quam.

Note to Parents and Teachers

The Healthy Teeth set supports national science standards related to personal health.
This book describes and illustrates healthy snacks for dental health. The images support
early readers in understanding the text. The repetition of words and phrases helps early
readers learn new words. This book also introduces early readers to subject-specific
vocabulary words, which are defined in the Glossary section. Early readers may need
assistance to read some words and to use the Table of Contents, Glossary, Read More,
Internet Sites, and Index sections of the book.

Table of contents

Good Snacks

Teresa eats good snacks.

They keep her teeth

and gums healthy

and strong.

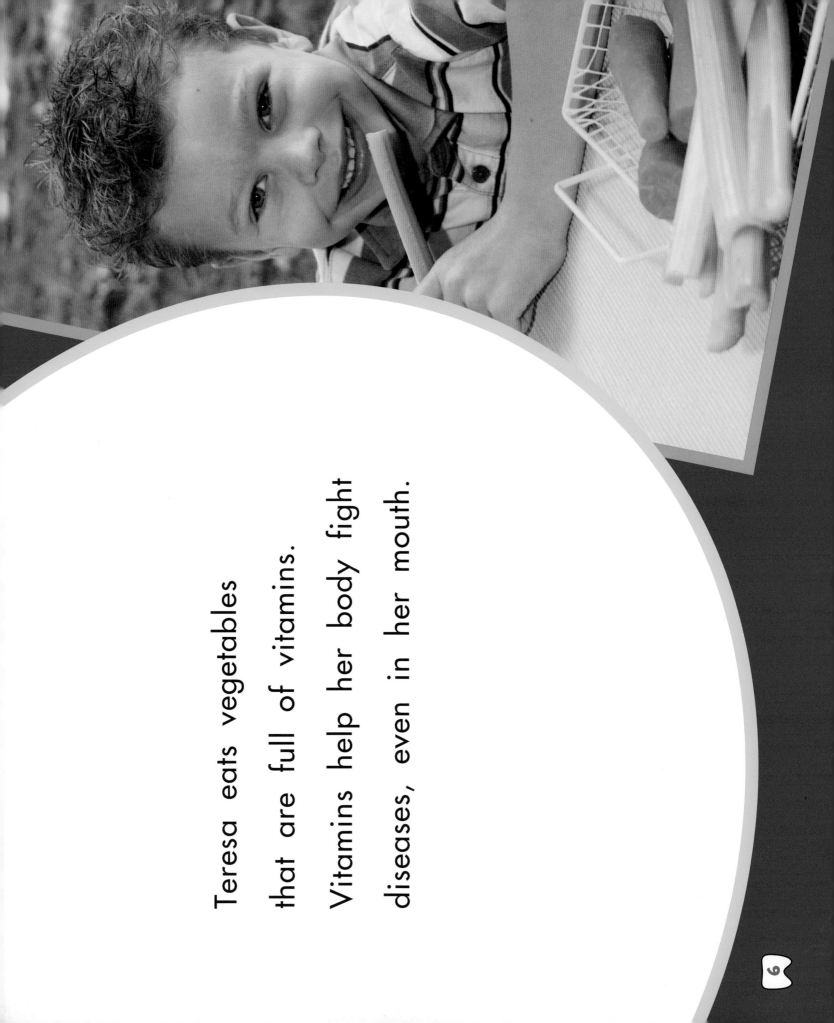

Teresa eats vegetables
that are full of vitamins.
Vitamins help her body fight
diseases, even in her mouth.

Teresa's mouth makes
more saliva when
she eats fresh fruit.
Saliva washes away sugar
that causes decay.

Teresa likes milk, cheese, and yogurt. These foods have calcium. Calcium makes teeth strong.

13

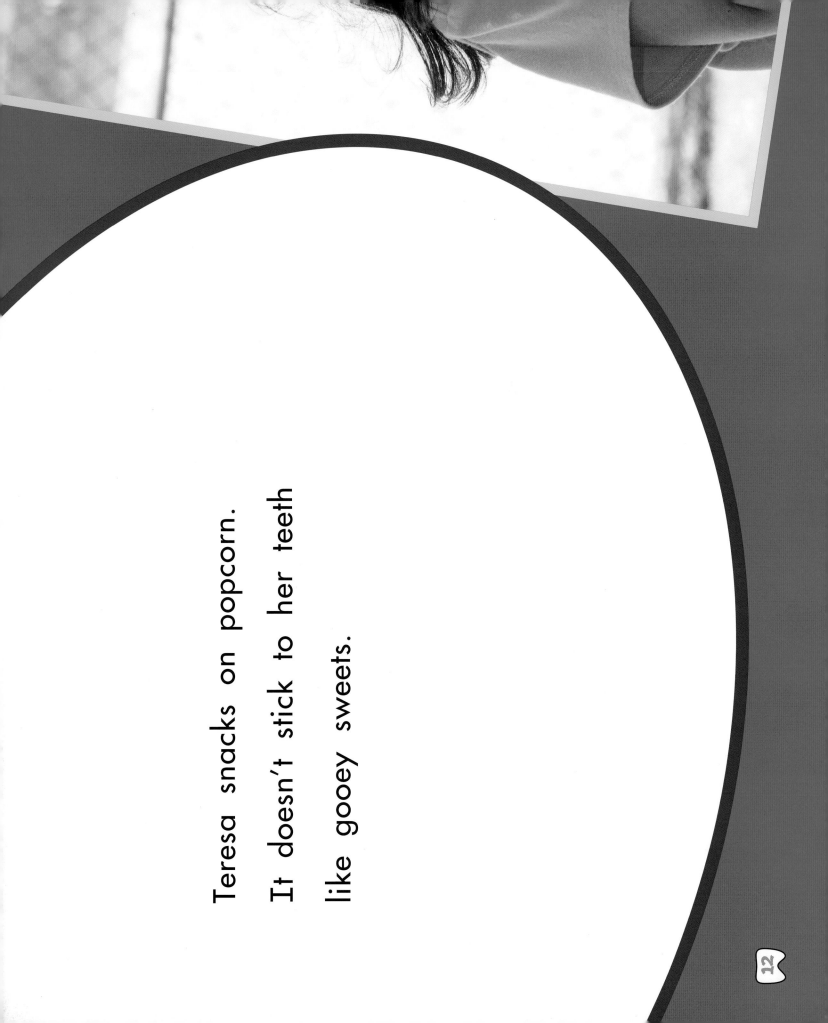

Teresa snacks on popcorn.

It doesn't stick to her teeth

like gooey sweets.

Sweets

Sweets like candy and soda

can hurt the enamel

that protects your teeth.

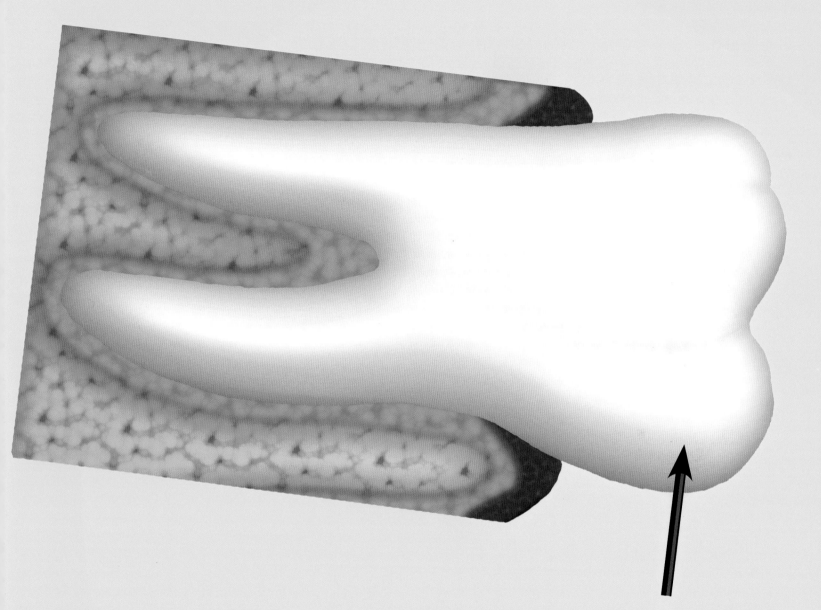

enamel

Germs in your mouth
turn sugar into acid.
Acid wears away enamel.
Acid causes decay
and cavities.

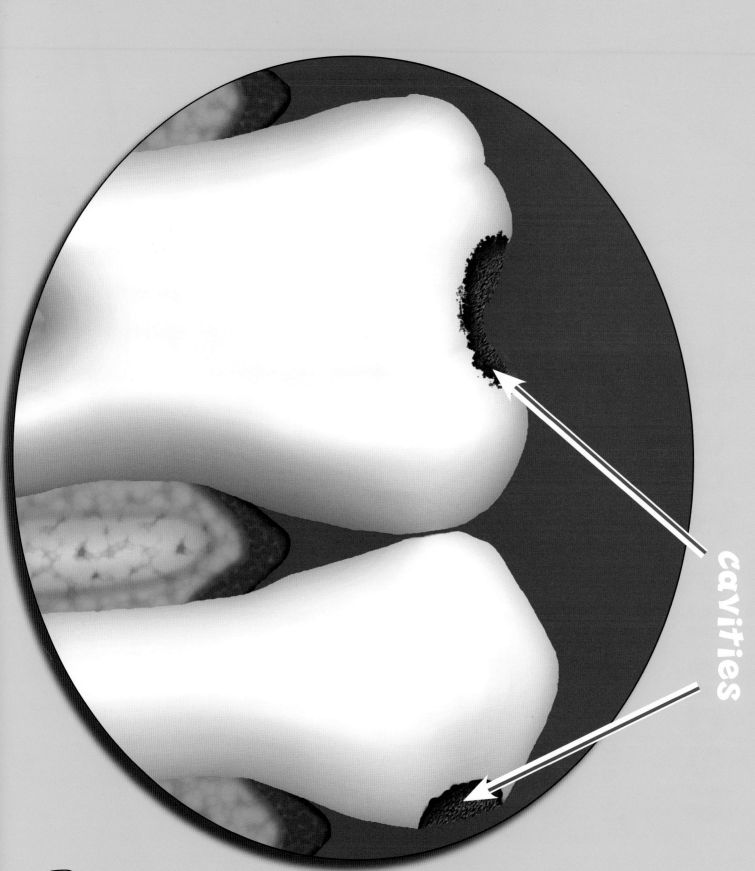

cavities

Healthy Teeth

Teresa brushes her teeth

to get rid of the acid.

Even rinsing

with water helps.

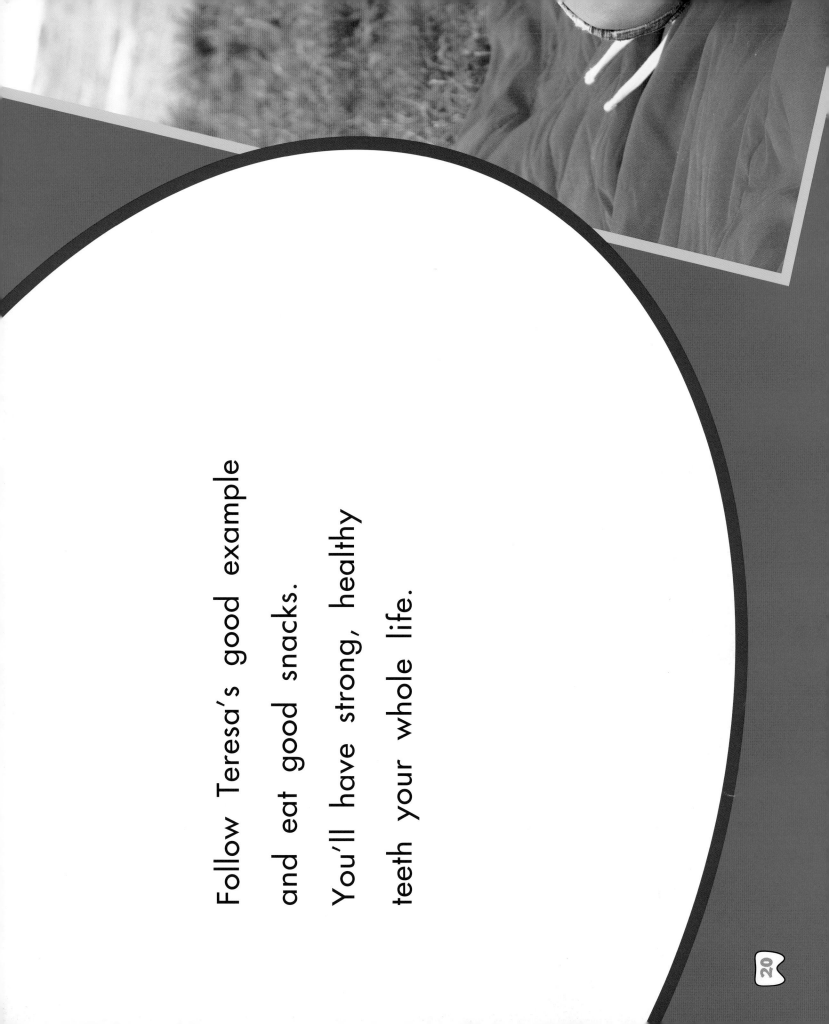

Follow Teresa's good example and eat good snacks.

You'll have strong, healthy teeth your whole life.

Glossary

acid — a liquid that wears away teeth; acid forms from germs and sugar in your mouth.

cavity — a decayed or broken-down part of a tooth; eating healthy snacks helps prevent cavities.

decay — to rot, break down, or make a hole in something

enamel — the hard, glossy covering on teeth; enamel protects teeth from decay.

gum — the firm skin around the base of teeth

saliva — the clear liquid in your mouth that keeps it moist, helps you swallow, and digest food

sweets — foods that have lots of sugar; candy, soft drinks, and cookies are sweets.

vitamin — a part of food that keeps you strong and helps protect you from getting sick

Read More

Kalman, Bobbie. *Super Snacks.* Kid Power. New York: Crabtree, 2003.

Royston, Angela. *Tooth Decay. It's Not Catching.* Chicago: Heinemann, 2004.

Schuh, Mari C. *Healthy Snacks.* Healthy Eating with MyPyramid. Mankato, Minn.: Pebble Books, 2006.

Internet sites

FactHound offers a safe, fun way to find Internet sites related to this book. All of the sites on FactHound have been researched by our staff.

Here's how:

1. Visit www.*facthound.com*

2. Choose your grade level.

3. Type in this book ID **1429612398** for age-appropriate sites. You may also browse subjects by clicking on letters, or by clicking on pictures and words.

4. Click on the **Fetch It** button.

FactHound will fetch the best sites for you!

Index

Word Count: 136
Grade: 1
Early-Intervention Level: 20